Where's Your Baby Brother, Becky Bunting?

By Hanne Tierney

Illustrated by Paula Winter

Doubleday & Company, Inc., Garden City, New York

ISBN: 0-385-08653-9 Trade
       0-385-08654-7 Prebound
Library of Congress Catalog Card Number 76–54474
Text copyright © 1979 by Hanne Tierney
Illustrations Copyright © 1978 by Paula Winter

9 8 7 6 5 4 3 2

Little Becky Bunting was a very sweet child.
She always said "please" and "thank you." She usually
played nicely by herself. And she liked to have
pleasant stories read to her—never anything with
violence or shooting. Becky didn't like any kind
of unpleasantness.

But one day something *very* unpleasant happened
to her. Her mother had a baby.

At first Becky tried to ignore him. But that turned out to be impossible.

"Becky dear," her mother would say, "look how your little brother is growing up. Soon he'll be a real friend to you, someone you can play with." Such words always left Becky feeling slightly car-sick.

And it almost killed her when her father said,
"I wouldn't be surprised if our little fellow here
grew up to be President someday. Don't you agree,
Becky?" Becky did not agree at all, especially since
nobody ever understood anything the little brother said.

Before she knew it, Becky's brother had
celebrated his second birthday and had grown into
a terrible toddler.

One warm spring day Becky's mother took her children on a picnic outing in Riverside Park. When they stopped for a red light, Mrs. Bunting cried out, "Oh, look at the sweet little dog!" The sweet little dog was really quite ugly and bad-tempered, and it started barking at the stroller.

"Stop that at once, Celia," said Celia's owner, a young man with long blond hair. Becky thought it was too bad that Celia wasn't allowed to scare her brother a little, especially when her mother said to the man, "My son just *loves* dogs. It's too bad he doesn't have one of his own."

Just then a girl rode up on a brand-new blue bicycle. She almost crashed into the stroller, because she obviously had not yet learned how to use the brakes. Becky looked at the bike with great longing. In her head she heard her mother say, "My daughter just *loves* bicycles. It's too bad she doesn't have one of her own."

But instead Mrs. Bunting said sensibly, "You see, Becky? Bicycles in the city are such nuisance."

After a few more blocks they arrived at the park. Becky's friend Danny sat on a swing, waiting to show her a new swing trick. Danny's trick could be done with two people, which is useful when there is only one empty swing and two people waiting for it.

Becky thought it was a good trick as well. It had to do with Danny lying across the swing on his stomach and Becky sitting on his back.

As usual, however, Mrs. Bunting called out,
"Becky, take your brother for a walk. But be careful
with him. Remember, he's still small."

When they got to the swings, the little brother stretched out his arms and said, "Fing, fing."

"What did he say?" Danny asked.

Becky rolled her eyes up and explained, "He means 'swing.'"

Just then the girl on the blue bicycle rode into the playground.

Becky said, "I wish I had that bike."

"Me too," said Danny. "It has speeds."

Becky sighed. "Look at her," she said. "She is younger than we are, and she has a bike and we don't."

Danny kept swinging the little brother, but Becky kept an eye on the blue bicycle.

After a while the girl rode over to the swings. She patted Becky's brother on the head and said, "I wish I had a baby brother."

"How would you like to trade?" Becky asked quickly.

"Sure," said the girl. "What do you want for him?"

"Your bicycle," said Becky.

"It's a deal," said the girl. "You take my bike, and I'll stay here and swing your brother."

Becky took the bike and called out to Danny, "Hey, Danny, you can have a ride, too."

When Danny heard this, he forgot all about what he was doing. He let go of the little brother, who fell right off the swing. But the girl picked him up and talked to him in baby talk, which the little brother liked.

"She'll take good care of him," thought Becky, and she jumped onto her new bike.

A few minutes later Becky happened to be riding past the bench where her mother sat, talking to another mother.

"Where is your little brother, Becky?" Mrs. Bunting called in a worried voice. So, naturally, Becky told her about the fabulous trade she had just made. And how lucky she and Danny were to have a three-speed bicycle. And how well the girl took care of the little brother. But instead of being happy at the good news, Mrs. Bunting became hysterical.

"How could you do such a terrible thing, you bad child?" she said several times in a row. "We've got to look for this girl right away." And she yanked Becky's arm very hard.

Becky wished her arm would come off so her mother would be sorry. But there was nothing sorry about Mrs. Bunting. She was just plain furious.

She and Becky ran all over the playground looking for the girl and the little brother, but they couldn't find them. Instead they found a policeman. Mrs. Bunting told him what had happened, and he asked them to describe the little brother and the girl. Mrs. Bunting remembered everything about the little brother. But Becky remembered nothing about the little girl except her sneakers, because they had hearts on them.

"You'd better go to the police station and wait there," said the policeman. Everybody followed him to a police car. Danny wanted to go too, but Mrs. Bunting wouldn't hear of it.

"After all," she said, "it isn't *your* fault Becky gave away her little brother. Why, we may never see him again."

This frightful thought made Mrs. Bunting cry loudly into her handkerchief.

To comfort her, the driver policeman told funny stories about lost children who turned up thirty years later with long beards and long hair and long fingernails. Mrs. Bunting did not think these stories were funny at all and kept right on crying.

When they arrived at the police station, all the policemen felt sorry for Mrs. Bunting. They brought her a cup of coffee, and after a little while she stopped crying.

But nobody brought anything for Becky, and she suddenly felt a big lump in her throat. She wondered if they would let her out of jail in time for Christmas.

Then the door opened and Becky's father walked in. The sight of her husband started Mrs. Bunting crying all over again. Mr. Bunting took her hands and said, "Don't worry, dear, the police will find him."

Then he did something very upsetting, and I am
sorry to have to mention it. He walked over to Becky
and gave her the biggest spanking of her life. Which
meant that now *both* Becky and her mother were crying.

All at once Mrs. Bunting jumped up and shouted, "I hear him! I hear him!" And she ran out into the hall.

The girl had brought back the little brother. She looked tired. Her nice sneakers were stepped on. Her face was dirty. A green lollipop was stuck in her hair, and Becky knew for sure that the little brother had put it there.

Mrs. Bunting kept hugging her son and saying, "Thank you, thank you" to the girl. But the girl just asked if she could please have her bicycle back.

A policeman brought in the bicycle, and Mrs. Bunting kissed the girl for returning the little brother. Then the Bunting family said "good-bye" and "thank you" to the policemen, and went home. And they almost forgot Becky, who sat on her chair and wished she could turn into a poisonous spider.

Later that evening Becky's father said he
was sorry about the spanking. And Becky said she
was sorry about trading her brother.

So Mr. and Mrs. Bunting forgave their daughter
Becky. Mrs. Bunting even made strawberry shortcake for
everyone's dessert.

Becky was allowed to stay up late and watch a scary show on television.

And the little brother only spilled Becky's crayons twice and only broke the red one.

The lesson of this story is really very simple:
Don't trade your little brother or your little sister
for anything. You will have nothing but trouble, and
they always come back in the end.